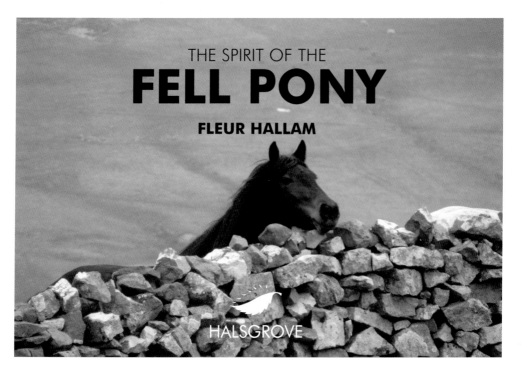

THE SPIRIT OF THE

FELL PONY

FLEUR HALLAM

HALSGROVE

First published in Great Britain in 2008

British Library Cataloguing-in-Publication Data
A CIP record for this title is available from the British Library

ISBN 978 1 84114 670 6

HALSGROVE
Halsgrove House
Ryelands Industrial Estate
Bagley Road, Wellington
Somerset TA21 9PZ
Tel: 01823 653777
Fax: 01823 216796
email: sales@halsgrove.com
website: www.halsgrove.com

Printed and bound by D'Auria Industrie Grafiche Spa, Italy

Introduction

Fell ponies have always been part of my life. When I was born my mother already owned and worked with them, and by the age of six I was riding a Fell mare called Peggy (Admergill Ursula). My enthusiasm for the breed grew even more when I spent some of my childhood in Cumbria, and I have never been without a Fell in my life since. Coming from an artistic family, and finding my creative gene flourished behind a camera, I decided to capture the spirit of these ponies in their native region.

This old breed of mountain pony has long roamed the hills of Cumberland and Westmorland, and their characteristics are a perfect match for their terrain. Breeders name their Fell studs after the farm, valley, or river they are located at, such as Tebay, Murthwaite, Greenholme, Sleddale, and Heltondale. With a height limit of 14 hands, they are sturdy and well-balanced with a long stride. Like all mountain ponies they are exceptionally alert, with big, bright eyes, large nostrils and small ears. The body is deep and well-muscled, the legs powerful and the hooves round with silky 'feather' (hair), mane, & tail. Fell ponies are black, brown, bay or grey, a star on the forehead, or white on or below the hind fetlock is allowed.

I dedicate this book to the hill breeders of Cumbria, whose commitment to the breed means semi-feral herds continue to roam the fells. The Fell Pony is an integral part of the region's natural beauty and must be safeguarded for future generations to enjoy and understand.

Riders and their ponies at the 150th Crosby Ravensworth Show.

Opposite page:
The 150th Crosby Ravensworth Show,
a successful day for Lownthwaite P & O.

Full winter coat: Bracklinn Red Lady enjoys some February sunshine at Stenkeld.

Opposite page:
Thinking of Spring: yearling filly Bybeck Georgie Girl.

Stallion Guards Jester
stands amongst lines
of dry stone
Lakeland walls.

Opposite page:
Broodmare, Hades Hill
Patience, grazing
peacefully.

Two-year-old colt Holling Cliffy shows his youthful cheekiness.

Opposite page: Greenholme Veronica and Lunesdale Mountain Heather in natural tandem.

Littletree yearling
colts enjoy an
afternoon play fight.

Opposite page:
High up on the fell side,
a Murthwaite mare
delights in a warm
spring breeze.

To new pastures, an early trot out on an April morning.

Half brothers together, yearling colts
Littletree Matador and Mountain Prince.

The native radiance of mare
Murthwaite Cloud on the fell side.

Naturally handsome:
Guards Jester.

Opposite page:
Murthwaite mares,
Irina, Blossom and
Fern, living naturally
on the Howgill fells.

17

Murthwaite fillies Dawn Chorus and Bracken's Lass share a moment together.

Murthwaite John Tom happily enjoys his relaxation.

A good fit: Bybeck Cherry Blossom stands beside a stone wall on a damp spring day.

Tranquility: Murthwaite Dusty in the spring sunshine.

Stepping out, yearling colt Greenholme Albert en route to winning his class.

Three-year-old colt Greenholme Warbler wins his class at the Stallion and Colt Show.

Two Lunesdale broodmares Blackbird and Gypsy Rose rest in the morning sunshine.

Judging the two-year-old colt class, Murthwaite Gurka impresses the judge to stand first.

Opposite page:
Proud mother, Bybeck Cherry Blossom, with her filly foal.

Stallion Wellbrow Rambler proudly shows off his flowing mane.

1st prize winner at the Stallion and Colt Show, Linnel Reynard is top of the seniors.

At Murthwaite yard:
stallion Look At Me
sniffs inquisitively
at a stable door.

Opposite page:
Wild beauty:
Murthwaite Rosebud.

Lowthnwaite Jimbo waits for his turn in the driven stallion class.

Opposite page:
Final placings: ridden stallions line up to collect
their rosettes, Severnvale Denzil in 1st place.

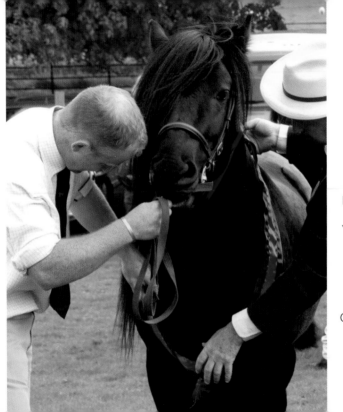

Putting the champions sash on, Carrock I'm Yer Man takes the title for the third time.

Opposite page:
Greenholme Stud foals silhouetted against a summer sky.

Stallion Murthwaite Windrush instinctively watches over his domain.

Filly Banksgate Black Gold being judged at the Fell Pony Society South Cumbria Show.

Watching showground activities, show winning mare Brackenbank Romany.

Opposite page:
First outing, a Carrock filly foal with her dam Townend Dawn II at the FPS South Cumbria Show.

A true showman, gelding Murthwaite Bracken.

Opposite page: Good all-rounder, ponies and their young riders stand in line during a Junior Ridden class.

Grey mare Lunesdale Mountain Music with fellow competitors during a Ridden class for mares.

Opposite page:
Broodmare Greenholme Crystal feeds her colt foal.

With tail in the air, Lownthwiate Tarmac
Adam feeds from his dam
Lownthwaite Otto Again.

Expectations of grass! Baronshill Bailey and
his handler at the FPS South Cumbria Show.

In unison, Townend Ruffle & Greenholme Kitty during a ridden pairs class.

The charm of youth,
foal Lownthwaite
Cashmere.

Opposite page:
Lownthwaite Fable and
colt foal Helios view
showground activities.

A happy occasion, Heltondale Misty IV gains her Olympia ticket at the 36th Breed Show.

Opposite page:
A line up of smart geldings. Judging the gelding 4–7 years old class at the 36th Breed Show.

At Waverhead Farm, mares Princess II and Jubilee
with their foals Poppy and Midnight Minstrel.

A contented moment: Murthwaite Cloud has a brief rest
on her breeder's shoulder during showing.

Foals Greenholme Bobby Dazzler and Brown Girl with broodmare Sleddale Megan.

Winning filly foal Greenholme Bethany with dam Greenholme Petal and family.

Youngstock Champion at the 36th Breed Show – yearling filly Brackenbank Gypsy III.

Heltondale Maydew enjoys a few moments of a soft summer breeze.

Burnhead Polly and colt foal Waverfoot JJ at home on a working farm.

Keeping the tradition, Severnvale Grey Bobby
put to a trade turnout at the 36th FPS Breed Show.

Opposite page:
Good companions: colt foals Greenholme Bracken and Bimbo.

Murthwaite Rosy and her filly foal graze amongst the buttercups in the shadow of the Howgills.

Natural beauties: Greenholme Fingers and foal, behind stands Heltondale Poppy and foal.

A Murthwaite colt rests in the summer sun, while his dam Murthwaite Irina grazes.

A picture of innocent youth, colt foal
Greenholme Hairy Harry.

Winners of the 36th Breed Show costume
class, Orton Hall Dennis & family.

Mares in the distance attract the attention
of stallion Lownthwaite Gary.

Opposite page:
Standing Supreme Champion: Rackwood Magic
at the 36th Fell Pony Breed Show.

A Murthwaite colt stretches out in the August sunshine.

Opposite page:
The grace of grey: Stallion Murthwaite Windrush
revels in a springtime gallop.

Follow me: Murthwaite Bonny Lad goes after his dam Heltondale Bonny Girl